I am Zach:
Mommy's Little

"A heartfelt story of deep love for a child with Autism and being truly Ausome in their own way"

I am Zach: Mommy's Little Ausome

"A story of deep love for a child with Autism and being truly Ausome in your own way"

Written by Zandra Mae Cochrane

All rights reserved. No part of this book may be reproduced, stored in a retrieval system, or transmitted in any form or by any means—electronic, mechanical, photocopying, recording, or otherwise—without prior written permission of the publisher.

ISBN: 978-1-7644630-9-6
Printed in Australia
First edition, 2025

To my Ausome Zach —
you are my joy, my wonder, and my greatest teacher.

Thank you for showing me a world filled with colour, courage, and love.

I am proud of you in every way, every day.
This book is for you, my little Ausome,
and for every child who shines in their own beautiful way.

What Ausome Means

"Ausome" is a word that blends Autism and awesome.

It celebrates the unique strengths, perspectives, and beautiful ways children on the spectrum experience the world.

Being Ausome means:
- seeing things differently
- learning in your own rhythm
- shining in your own way
- being valued exactly as you are

Every Ausome child brings something special to the world — and this heartfelt book is a celebration of that truth.

Author's Note

I chose the word "Ausome" because it reflects how I see my son — wonderfully unique, beautifully different, and full of strengths that deserve to be celebrated.

As a mother, I wanted a word that honours Autism with love, pride, and positivity. "Ausome" reminds us that every child has their own way of learning, growing, and shining.

This heartfelt story is my way of sharing that message with other families, educators, and anyone who walks alongside an Ausome child. May it bring comfort, understanding, and a little more light to your journey.

With love,
Mommy

Different but never less

Zach, my sweet boy,
from the moment you came,

I knew life would sparkle...

When you were little, the world felt so new,

And you saw it in colours I never quite knew.

You didn't use words the same way as the rest,

But you spoke with your laughter —
and that was the best.

You talked with your eyes,
with your hands,
with your play,

And Mommy learned all of your language each day.

Sometimes it's hard when you grew quiet and felt sick and weak,

Mommy got scared —
too frightened to speak

But you fought it all,
so brave and so small,

My strong little warrior conquered it all.

As you grew older, you blossomed with grace,

Exploring the world at your own gentle pace.

Some people looked and said
"you are different among the rest"
while
a doctor had whispered to my ears and said "Autism,"

But Mommy have learned to say "ausome" to your Autism instead of awesome because that's what she knows and felt in her heart.

For mommy,
Ausome means different in the most special way,

Ausome means shining a bit brighter each day.

Ausome means seeing the world through the lens and sparkles of your eyes,

Finding magic in places that others pass by.

And slowly, so slowly, like seeds growing under the rain and sun,

Your words started blooming — one by one.

Now you talk and giggle and even tell silly jokes,

You're funny and clever with all kinds of folks.

Though Mommy lives, and worked so far
and
don't see each other much,

She calls you in the line with so much love and touch.

Because she knew you brighten her day and wiped all the tiredness she got from work everyday.

You grow in your own way — not fast and not slow, Just perfectly Zach, in the way that you grow.

Some days are loud, and some feelings are strong, Don't worry, mommy is here and will walk with you all along.

You're brave, you're kind,
you're wonderfully true,
And Mommy is endlessly
proud of you.

Zach, my little Ausome, you shine like the sun, .
And I'll love you forever — my special awesome or ausome one.

Every child grows in their own beautiful way. This is Zach's story — a journey of strength, joy, and being truly Ausome.

From quiet beginnings to blooming words, from brave battles to silly giggles, Zach shines with a magic all his own.

With deep love and gentle hope, Zach, Mommy's Little Ausome celebrates neurodiversity, uniqueness, and the unbreakable bond between a mother and her child.

This heartwarming story helps children understand that being different is something to be proud of — because being Ausome means being wonderfully, uniquely you.

Let's Connect!

Create with Zandy

COLOURFUL STORIES FOR GROWING HEARTS

 @CREATEWITHZANDY

 ZANDRAMAECOCHRANEBOOKS.COM

 ZANDRAMAECOCHRANE@GMAIL.COM

 0432955276

www.ingramcontent.com/pod-product-compliance
Lightning Source LLC
Chambersburg PA
CBRC091503220426
43661CB00021B/1304